Hidden Pictures Practice Book

Pre K–Grade K
Ages 4 to 6

PRODIGYWIZARD
BOOKS

All Rights reserved. No part of this book may be reproduced or used in any way or form or by any means whether electronic or mechanical, this means that you cannot record or photocopy any material ideas or tips that are provided in this book

Copyright 2016

Help me find the hidden pictures!

HELP ME FIND THESE!

HELP ME FIND THESE!

HELP ME FIND THESE!

HELP ME **FIND** THESE!

HELP ME FIND THESE!

HELP ME FIND THESE!

HELP ME FIND THESE!

HELP ME FIND THESE!

HELP ME **FIND** THESE!

HELP ME FIND THESE!

HELP ME FIND THESE!

HELP ME FIND THESE!

HELP ME **FIND** THESE!

HELP ME FIND THESE!

HELP ME FIND THESE!

ANSWERS!

HELP ME FIND THESE!

HELP ME FIND THESE!

HELP ME FIND THESE!

HELP ME FIND THESE!

HELP ME FIND THESE!

HELP ME FIND THESE!

HELP ME FIND THESE!

HELP ME FIND THESE!

HELP ME FIND THESE!

HELP ME FIND THESE!

HELP ME FIND THESE!

HELP ME **FIND** THESE!

HELP ME **FIND** THESE!

HELP ME **FIND** THESE!

HELP ME **FIND** THESE!

HELP ME FIND THESE!

HELP ME FIND THESE!

HELP ME FIND THESE!

HELP ME FIND THESE!

HELP ME FIND THESE!

HELP ME FIND THESE!

HELP ME FIND THESE!

HELP ME FIND THESE!

HELP ME FIND THESE!

HELP ME FIND THESE!

HELP ME FIND THESE!

HELP ME FIND THESE!

Printed in the USA
CPSIA information can be obtained
at www.ICGtesting.com
LVHW081505171124
796873LV00011B/630